LET'S
see

Groundhog Day

by Marc Tyler Nobleman

Content Adviser: Dr. S. Elwynn Taylor, Extension Meteorologist,
Professor of Agronomy, Iowa State University

Reading Adviser: Susan Kesselring, M.A., Literacy Educator,
Rosemount-Apple Valley-Eagan (Minnesota) School District

Let's See Library
Compass Point Books
Minneapolis, Minnesota

Compass Point Books
3109 West 50th Street, #115
Minneapolis, MN 55410

Visit Compass Point Books on the Internet at *www.compasspointbooks.com*
or e-mail your request to *custserv@compasspointbooks.com*

On the cover: Groundhog handler Bill Deeley presents Phil to the crowd February 2, 2002, during the annual Groundhog Day event in Punxsutawney, Pennsylvania.

Photographs ©: Chris Hondros/Getty Images, cover; Tim Boyle/Newsmakers/Getty Images, 4; Erwin and Peggy Bauer/Tom Stack & Associates, 6; Photo from Bill Anderson Collection, 8; Alan Freed/PunxsutawneyPhil.com, 10; Richard Cummins/Corbis, 12; Edward R. Degginger/Bruce Coleman Inc., 14; Licensed under the authority of the Town of South Bruce Peninsula, Ontario, Canada, owner of the offical marks "WIARTON WILLIE™", 16; Reuters NewMedia Inc./Corbis, 18; Archie Carpenter/Getty Images, 20.

Creative Director: Terri Foley
Managing Editor: Catherine Neitge
Editors: Brenda Haugen and Christianne Jones
Photo Researcher: Marcie C. Spence
Designers: Melissa Kes and Les Tranby
Educational Consultant: Diane Smolinski

Library of Congress Cataloging-in-Publication Data
Nobleman, Marc Tyler.
  Groundhog Day / by Marc Tyler Nobleman.
    v. cm. — (Let's see)
  Includes bibliographical references and index.
  Contents: What is Groundhog Day?—What is a groundhog?—Where does the main Groundhog Day event take place?—What happens on Groundhog Day?—How did Groundhog Day begin?—How did Groundhog Day come to the United States?—How accurate are the groundhog's predictions?—Who else predicts the weather on Groundhog Day?—What does Groundhog Day mean to people?
  ISBN 0-7565-0648-4 (hardcover)
  1. Groundhog Day—Juvenile literature. [1. Groundhog Day. 2. Holidays.] I. Title. II. Series.
  GT4995.G76N63 2005
  394.261—dc22   2003023608

Table of Contents

*NOTE: In this book, words that are defined in the glossary
are in **bold** the first time they appear in the text.*

What Is Groundhog Day?

Groundhog Day is a festival in the United States and Canada. People believe an animal called a groundhog **predicts** the weather on Groundhog Day. They watch as the groundhog comes out of its hole after **hibernating.**

According to an old story, if the groundhog sees its shadow, winter will last six more weeks. If the groundhog does not see its shadow, spring will begin soon.

Groundhog Day is February 2. Schools, post offices, banks, government offices, and companies do not close on Groundhog Day.

◄ *A groundhog at an Illinois zoo casts a shadow as she enjoys a snack.*

What Is a Groundhog?

A groundhog is a type of **rodent.** Mice, squirrels, and beavers are rodents, too. The groundhog also is called a woodchuck, marmot, or whistle pig.

Groundhogs live in woods and **ravines** in the United States and Canada. They are plump and furry. Their fur is often brown.

Groundhogs' bodies are about 2 feet (60 centimeters) long. They weigh about 13 pounds (6 kilograms) and have bushy tails that are about 6 inches (15 centimeters) long.

Groundhogs search for food during the day and sleep at night. They are **herbivores.** They eat leaves, flower stems, tree bark, and berries.

◄ *A groundhog chews on a flower stem.*

Where Does the Main Groundhog Day Event Happen?

In 1886, Clymer Freas said February 2 would be Groundhog Day. He worked at a Pennsylvania newspaper called *The Punxsutawney Spirit.* Freas printed the first announcement of Groundhog Day in this newspaper. Since then, Groundhog Day has been a yearly **tradition** in the United States.

Punxsutawney, Pennsylvania, became the center of Groundhog Day events. The groundhog that predicts the weather there every year is named Punxsutawney Phil. He is not a wild animal. Phil lives at the library.

◄ *Clymer Freas*

What Happens on Groundhog Day?

Thousands of people gather in Punxsutawney on Groundhog Day to see Phil predict the weather.

Phil is taken to a hill called Gobbler's Knob on this special day. He is placed in a warm **burrow** under a fake tree stump. At 7:25 A.M., Phil is pulled out of his burrow while the crowd watches. An official puts Phil to his ear so the groundhog can whisper his prediction. It is just pretend, but everyone likes the show. The official says whether or not Phil saw his shadow.

People across the country watch the fun on television. People also celebrate Groundhog Day with games, dancing, eating, and sleigh rides.

◄ *Officials look at Phil as they lift him away from his tree stump.*

How Did Groundhog Day Begin?

Some of the Groundhog Day traditions come from old festivals called Imbolc and Candlemas.

Imbolc was celebrated long ago in Ireland. Around Imbolc, farm animals gave birth, and grass popped up through the snow. Candlemas was an old **Christian** festival held in Europe on February 2. The Christians believed that if Candlemas day was sunny, then winter would go on. If Candlemas was rainy, they thought spring would arrive soon.

Both of these festivals took place in midwinter. During both festivals, people watched for the coming of spring. Also, animals were important on both festivals.

◄ *Winter frost turns the ground and trees white in a park in Ireland.*

How Did Groundhog Day Come to the United States?

Long ago, European people added an animal tradition to Candlemas. They said if the animal saw its shadow on Candlemas, winter would last six more weeks. If the animal did not see its shadow, it was a sign of spring. Europeans used the hedgehog, the badger, or the bear as the special animal.

In the 1700s, many Germans came to live in Pennsylvania. They brought the Candlemas tradition with them. They found no hedgehogs or badgers, but they saw plenty of groundhogs. The Germans began to use groundhogs to predict the weather on Candlemas.

◄ *A badger looks around a springtime field.*

Who Else Predicts the Weather on Groundhog Day?

Punxsutawney Phil isn't the only animal that predicts the weather on Groundhog Day. Birmingham Bill is a groundhog at the Birmingham Zoo in Alabama that predicts the weather. Buckeye Chuck is a groundhog that makes a prediction in Ohio. Dunkirk Dave and Malverne Mel are in New York. Jimmy is in Wisconsin, a state that calls itself the Groundhog Capital of the World.

In Louisiana, a crawfish named Claude predicts the weather! In Canada, Shubenacadie Sam and Wiarton Willie are two popular groundhogs that predict weather. Willie has white fur.

◀ *Wiarton Willie predicts the weather in Wiarton, Ontario.*

How Often Is the Groundhog Right?

On Groundhog Day, an official tells a crowd what Punxsutawney Phil predicted. If the groundhog predicts a long winter, people are disappointed. If he predicts an early spring, they are happy.

Phil is not always right. People have kept records of Phil's predictions for all but nine years since 1887. Between 1887 and 2004, Phil saw his shadow 94 times. He did not see his shadow 14 times. However, Phil has been right less than half the time. He is not the best weatherman!

◄ *The Groundhog Day celebration in Punxsutawney, Pennsylvania*

What Does Groundhog Day Mean to People?

Groundhog Day is full of fun. In the United States and Canada, it is the only well-known festival named for a **mammal.** Groundhog Day is a great day for animal lovers. People think the groundhog is cute and like to watch him.

People do not really believe a groundhog can predict the weather. However, the groundhog is a **symbol** to many people. They hope that spring is coming quickly to end winter's cold days.

The weather-telling groundhog is an old tradition that is still fun today.

◄ *Some people dress up in silly costumes on Groundhog Day.*

Glossary

ancestral—having to do with an ancestor, a member of a person's family who lived a long time ago

burrow—a tunnel or hole made or used by an animal

Christian—the faith that believes Jesus Christ is the son of God

herbivores—animals that eat plants

hibernating—resting or sleeping for the winter

mammal—a warm-blooded animal that grows hair; female mammals produce milk for their young

predicts—tells beforehand what will happen

ravines—deep, narrow valleys

rodent—a kind of four-legged animal, such as a mouse, with long teeth for gnawing

symbol—something that stands for something else

tradition—a custom that is common among a family or group

Did You Know?

* Groundhogs dig dens that may have several rooms. They also may make several entrances into the dens.
* The word woodchuck comes from the Delaware Indian word *wojak*. According to an Indian story, the Delaware's **ancestral** grandfather was a wojak, or groundhog.

* Some farmers think groundhogs are pests because they can damage crops.
* Punxsutawney calls itself The Weather Capital of the World.
* As many as 30,000 people go to the Groundhog Day festivities in Punxsutawney.

Want to Know More?

In the Library

Arno, Iris Hiskey. *The Secret of the First One Up.* Chanhassen, Minn.: NorthWord Press, 2003.

Becker, Michelle Aki. *Groundhog Day*. New York: Children's Press, 2003.

Freeman, Don. *Gregory's Shadow.* New York: Viking, 2000.

Gerard, Valerie J. *Spring: Signs of the Season Around North America.* Minneapolis: Picture Window Books, 2003.

On the Web

For more information on *Groundhog Day,* use FactHound to track down Web sites related to this book.

1. Go to *www.facthound.com*
2. Type in a search word related to this book or this book ID: 0756506484.
3. Click on the *Fetch It* button.

Your trusty FactHound will fetch the best Web sites for you!

On the Road

Groundhog Zoo at the Punxsutawney Memorial Library
301 E. Mahoning St.
Punxsutawney, PA 15767
The year-round home of Punxsutawney Phil and other groundhogs

Gobbler's Knob
Punxsutawney, PA 15767
The wooded site of Punxsutawney Phil's annual weather forecast

Index

About the Author

Marc Tyler Nobleman has written more than 40 books for young readers. He has also written for a History Channel show called "The Great American History Quiz" and for several children's magazines including *Nickelodeon*, *Highlights for Children*, and *Read* (a Weekly Reader publication). He is also a cartoonist, and his single panels have appeared in more than 100 magazines internationally. He lives in Connecticut.